Vol 5

MAZE

Ages 4-6

FOR KIDS

MAZE BOOK

SOCIAL MEDIA

/MySweetBooks1

/MySweetBooks1

/MySweetBooks1

/MySweetBooks

Email Us : mysweetbooks1@gmail.com

Milk

MILK

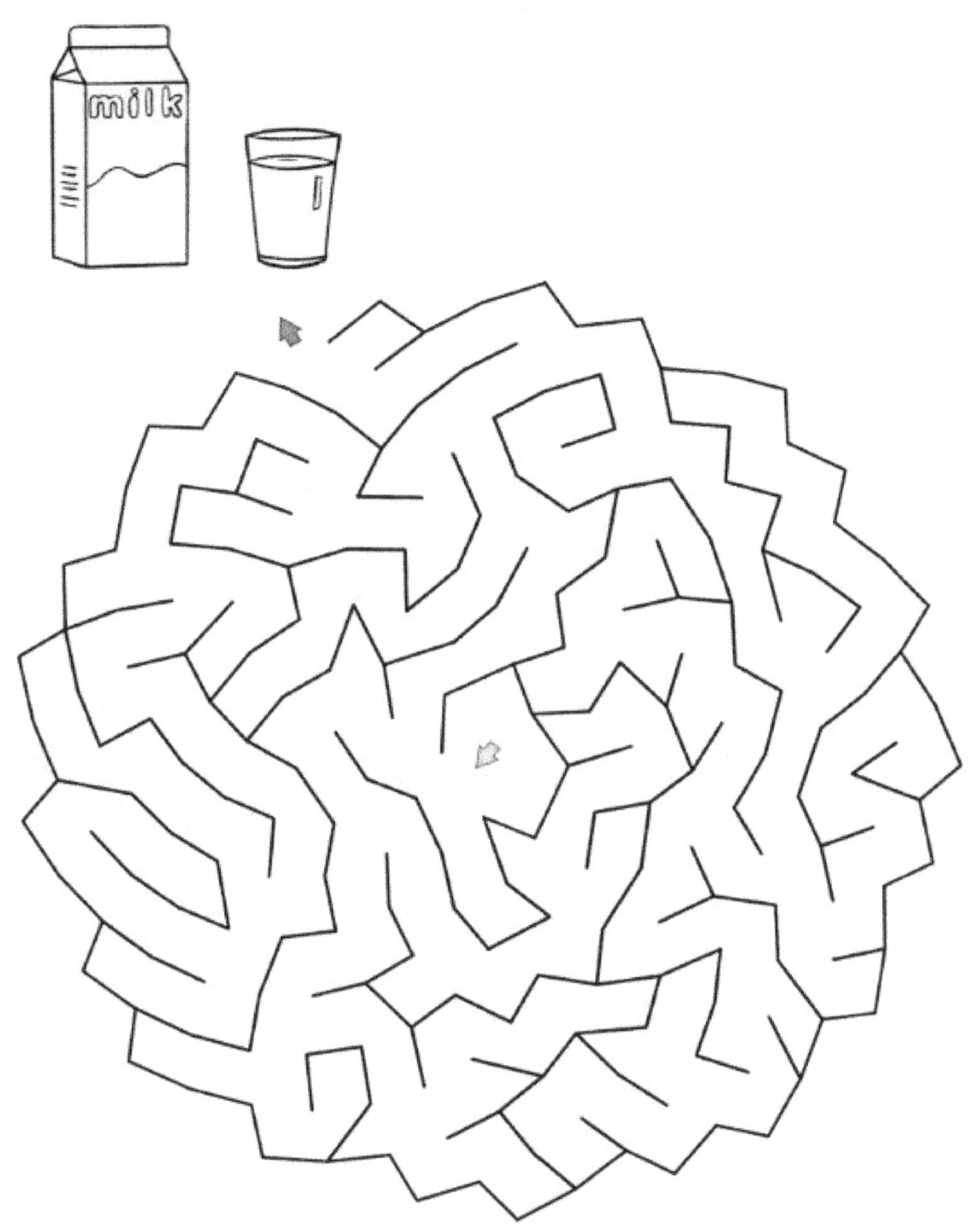

Milk

MILK

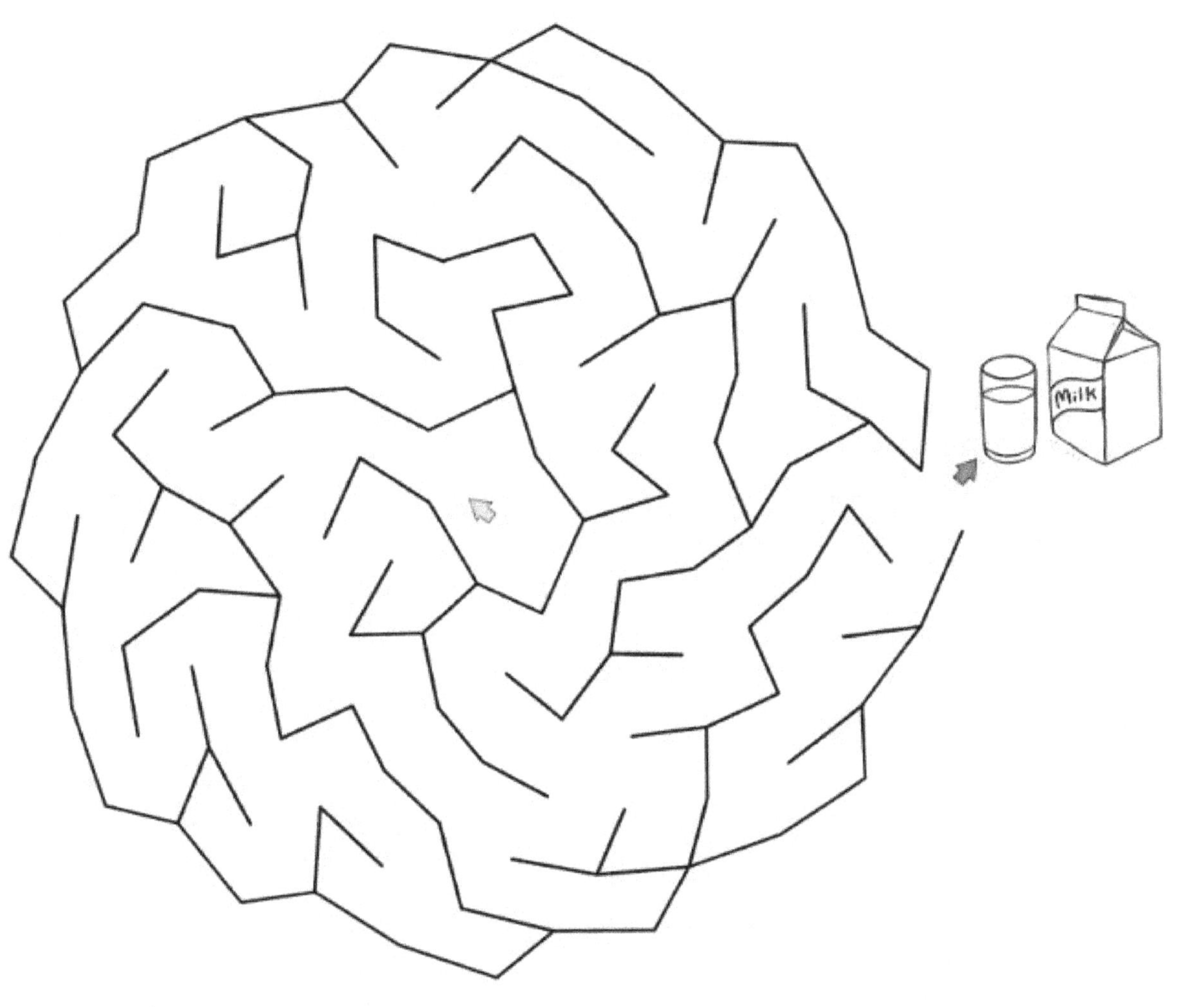
Milk

milk

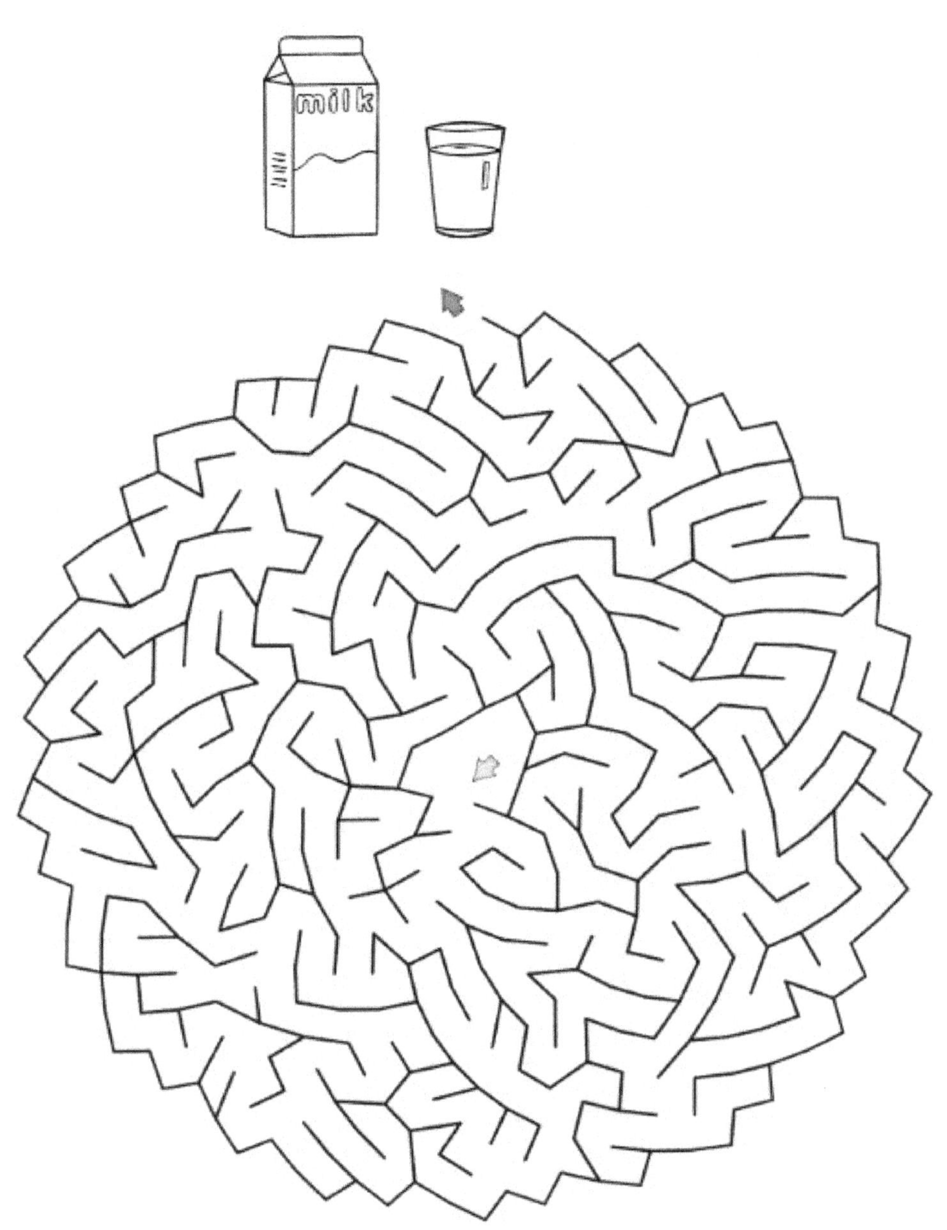

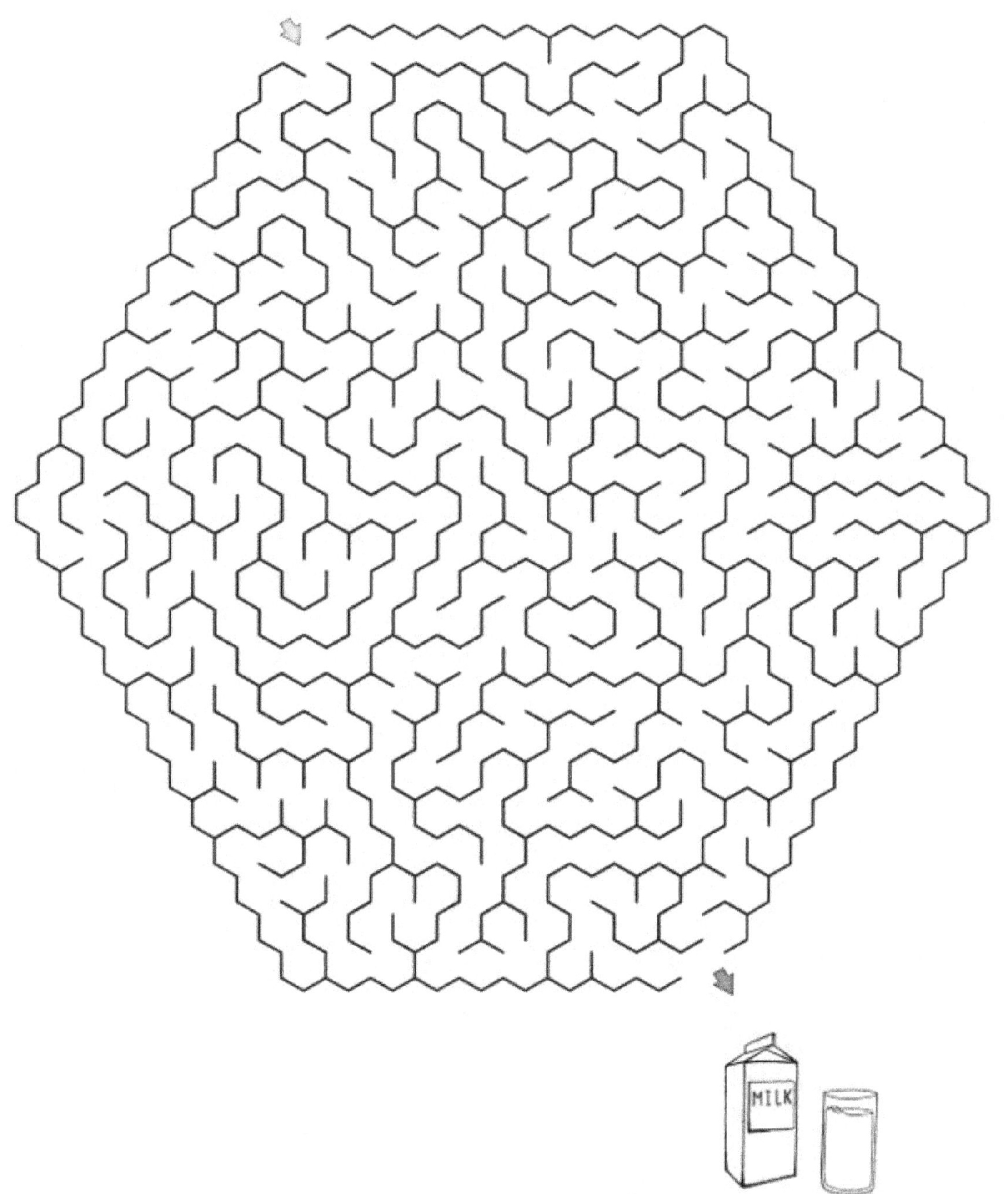

Milk

Milk

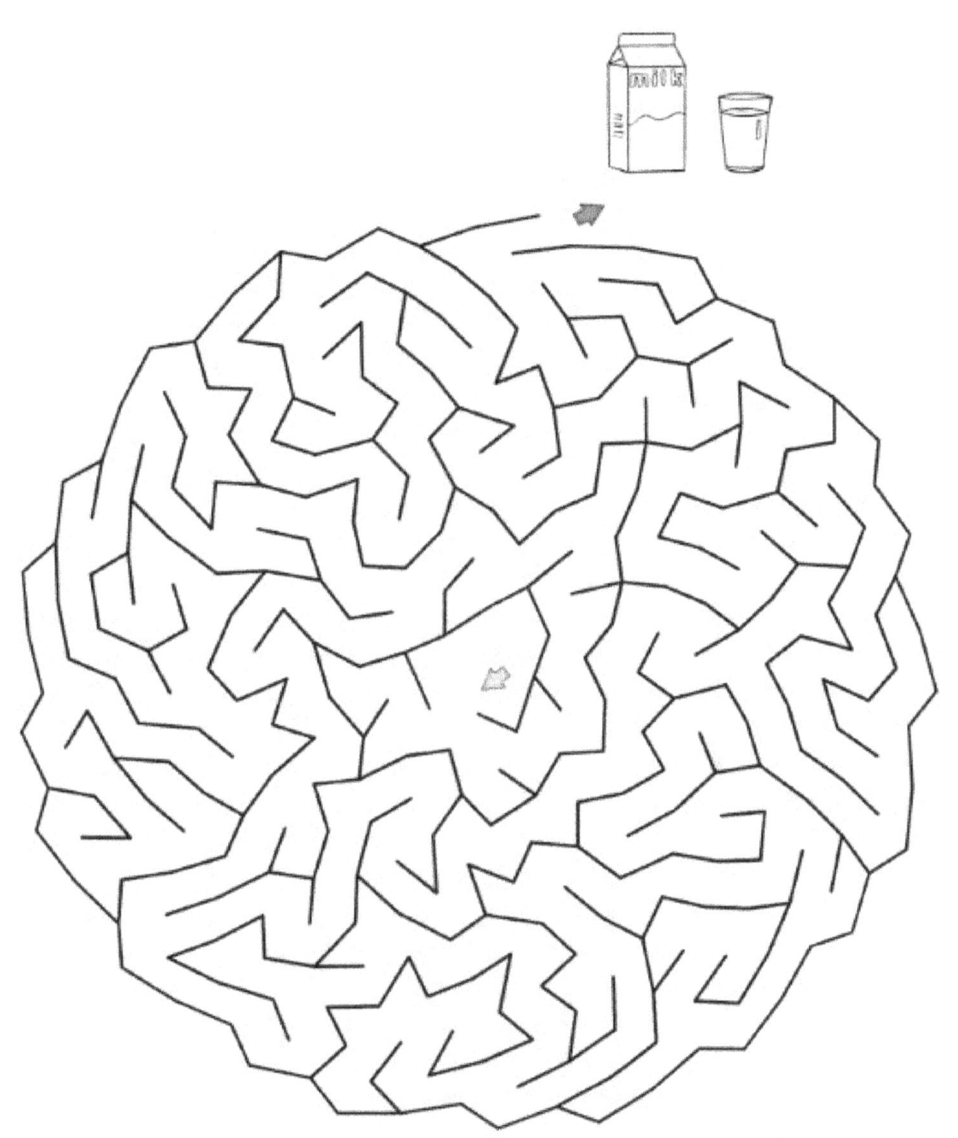

Milk

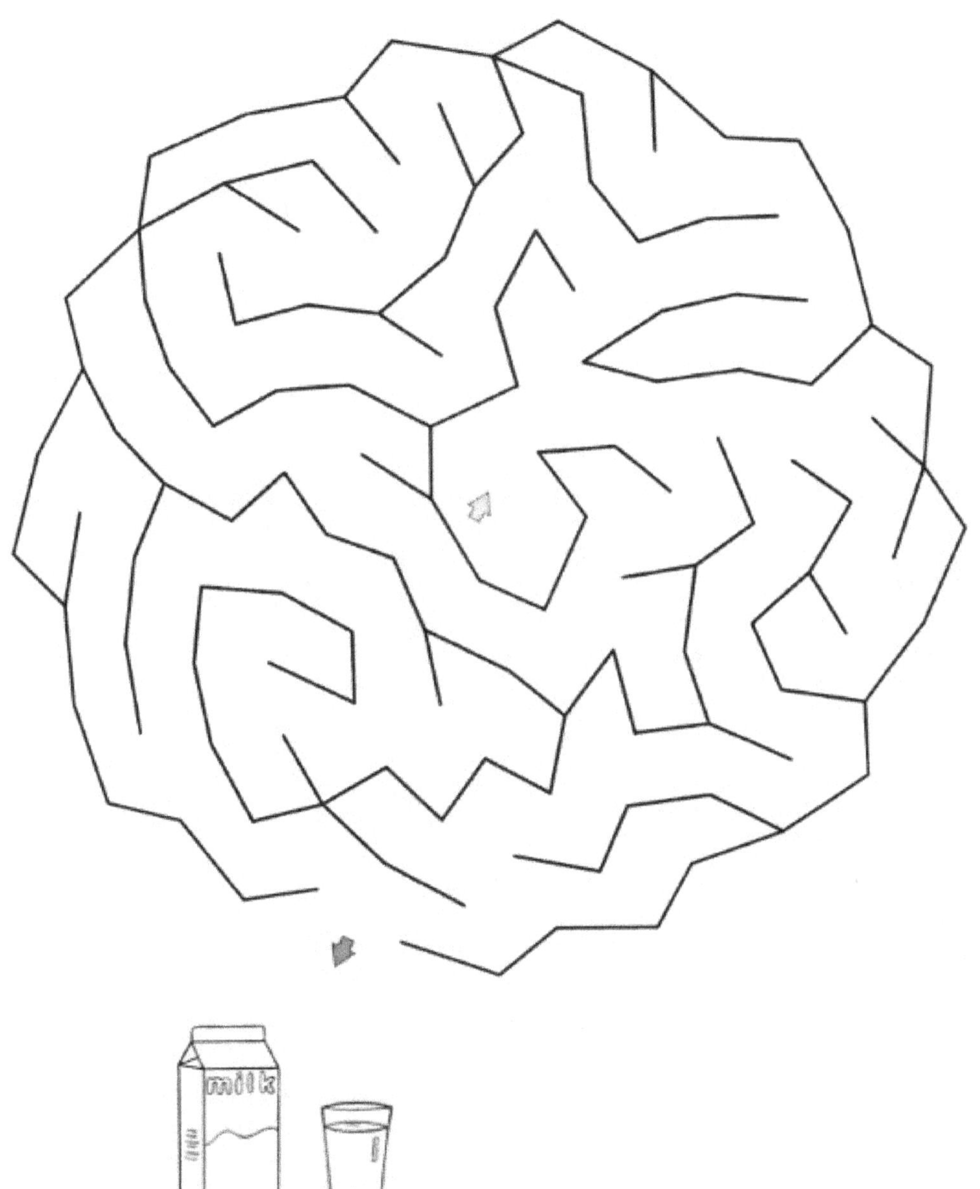

MILK

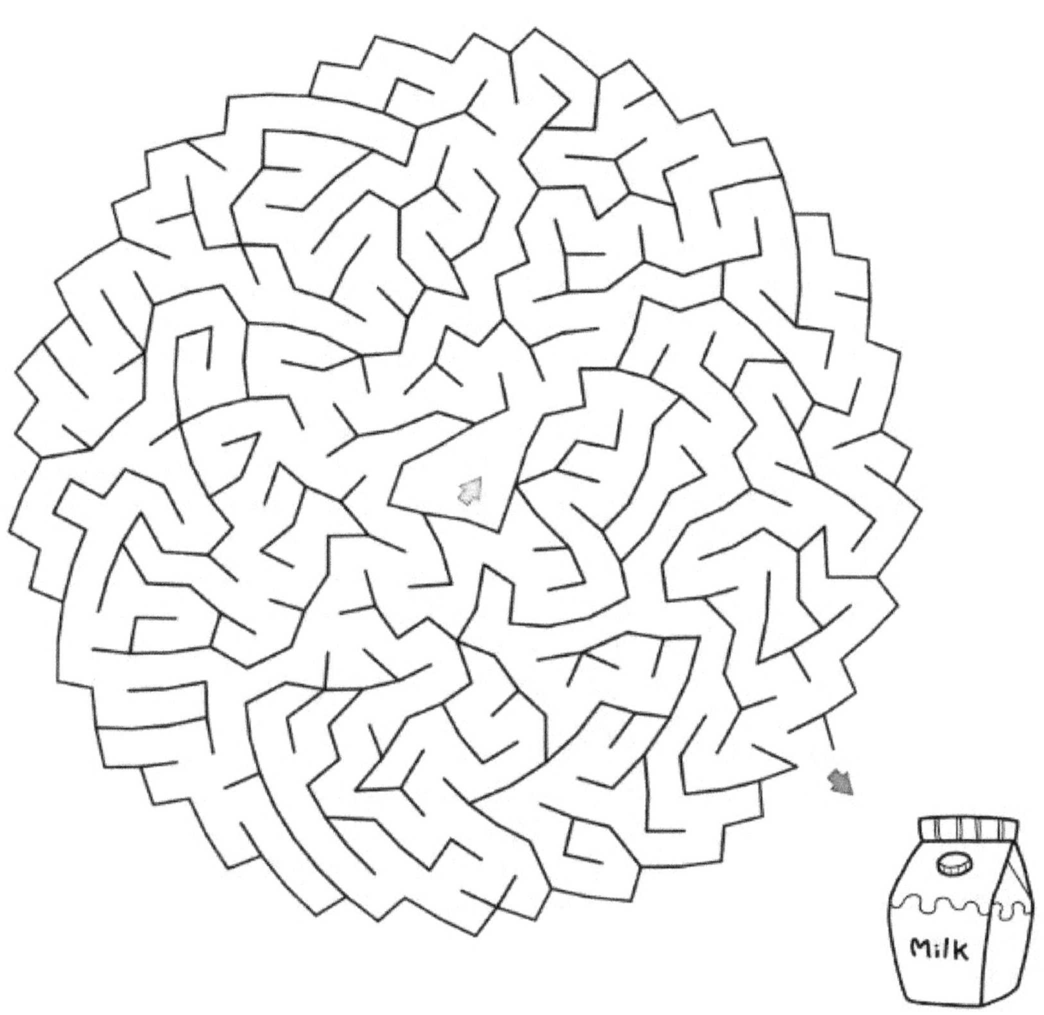
Milk

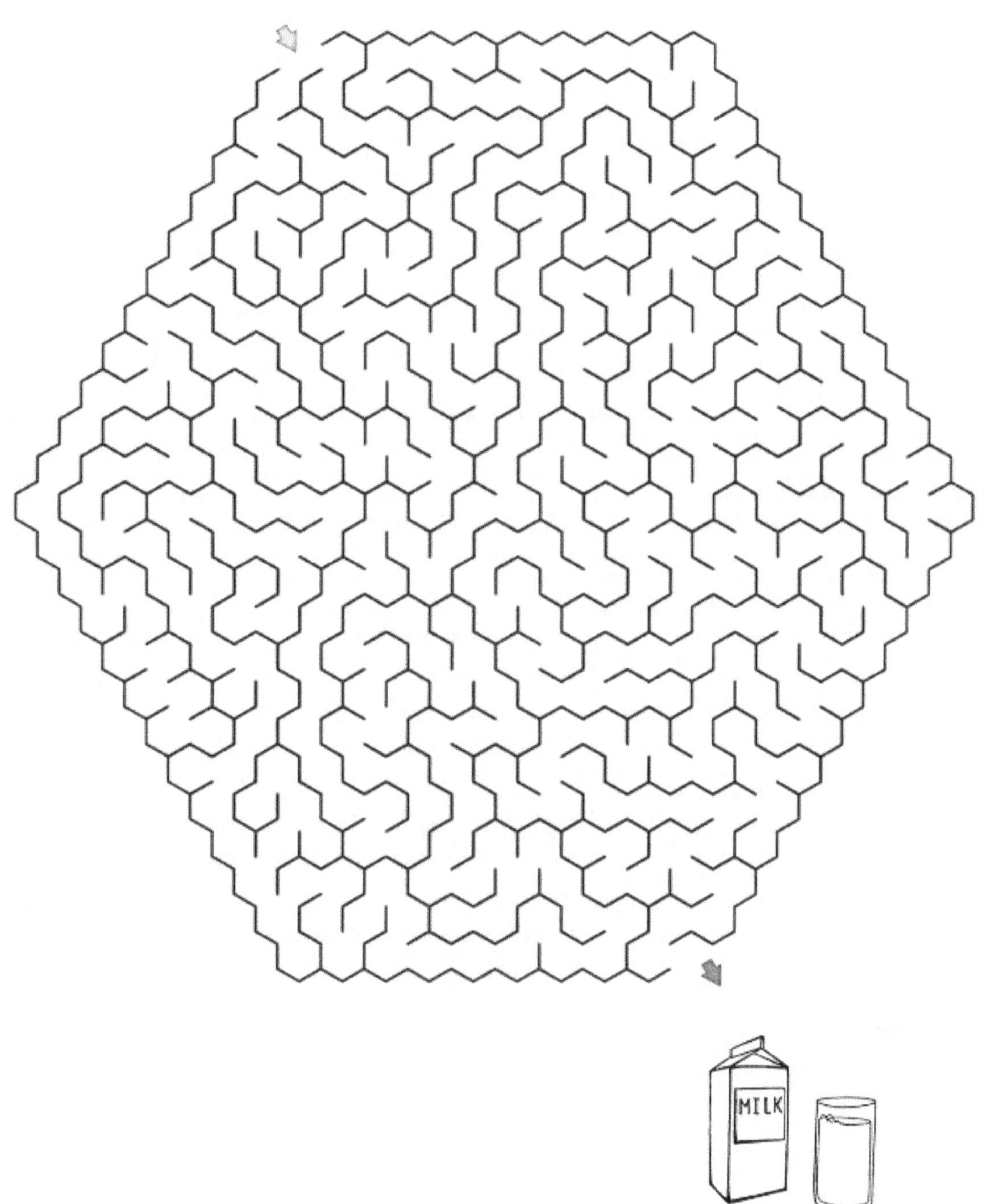

milk

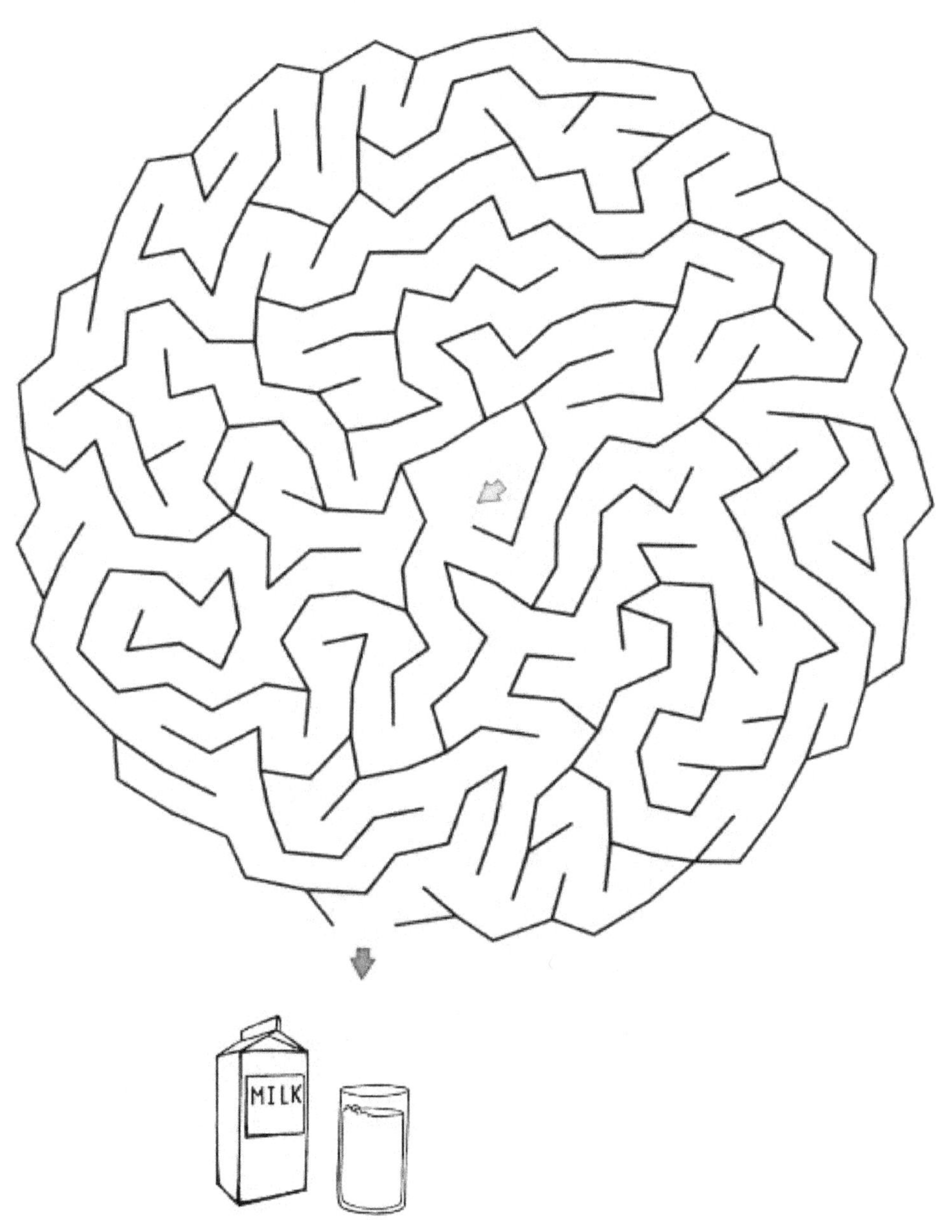
MILK

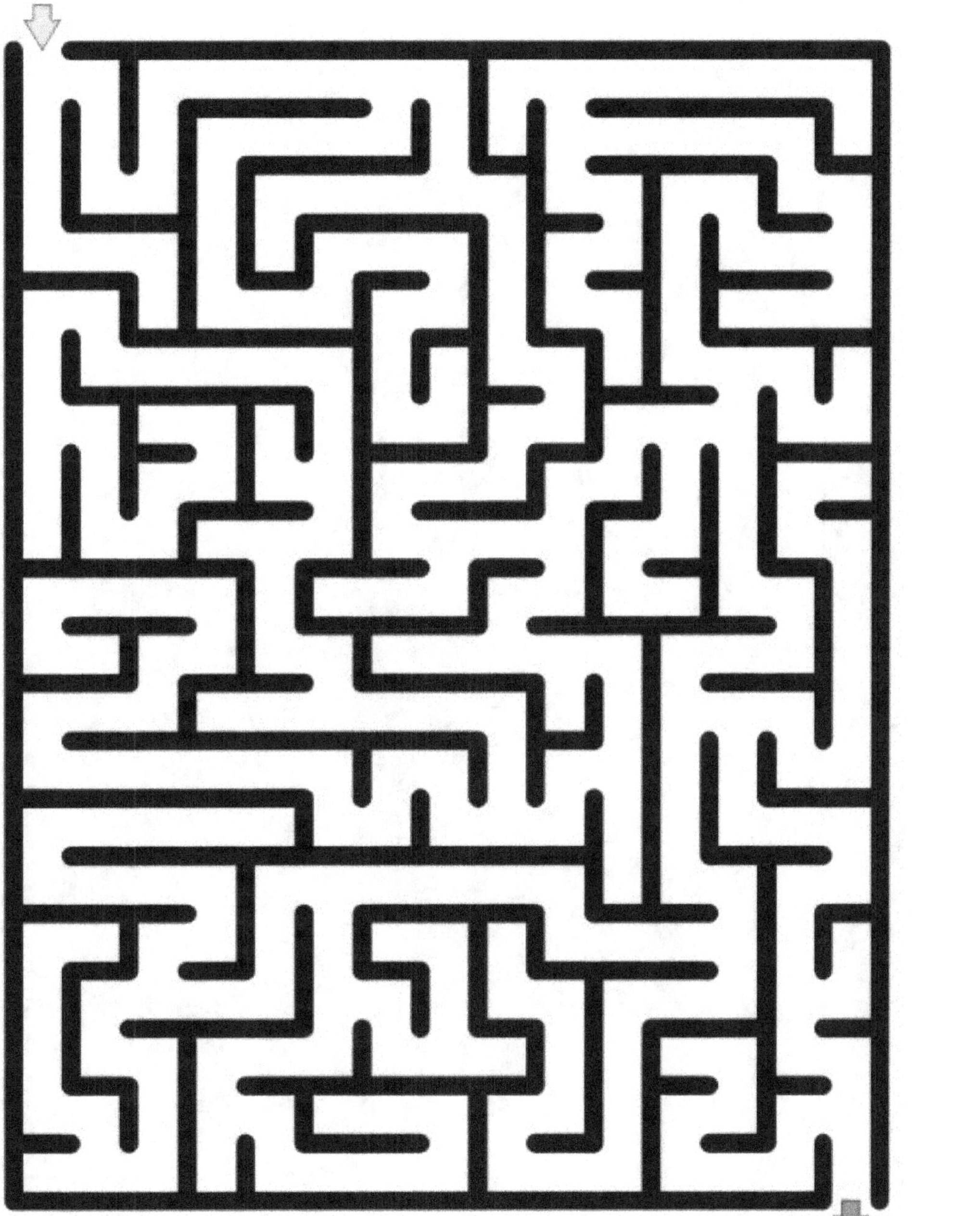

Milk

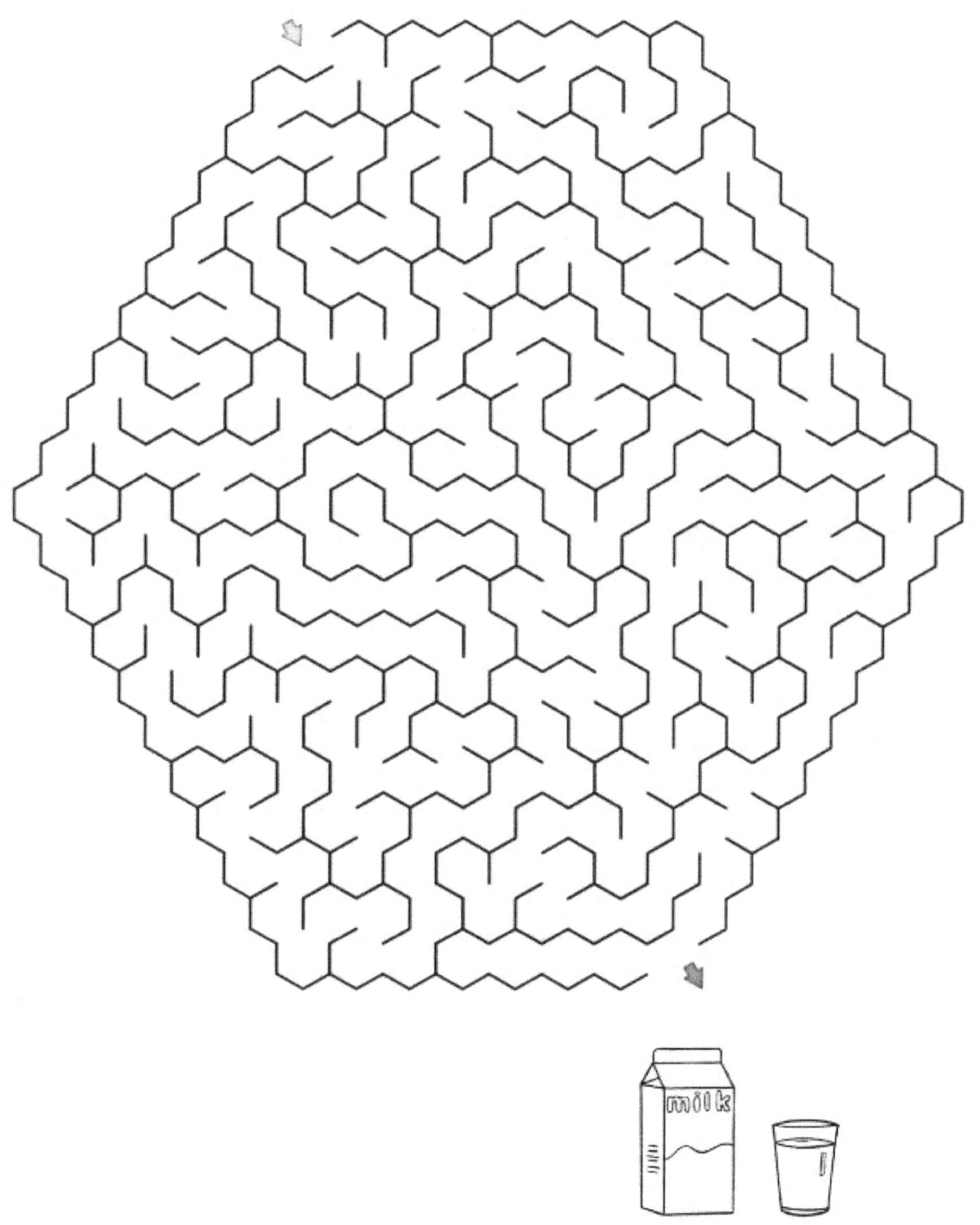

Milk

Milk

milk

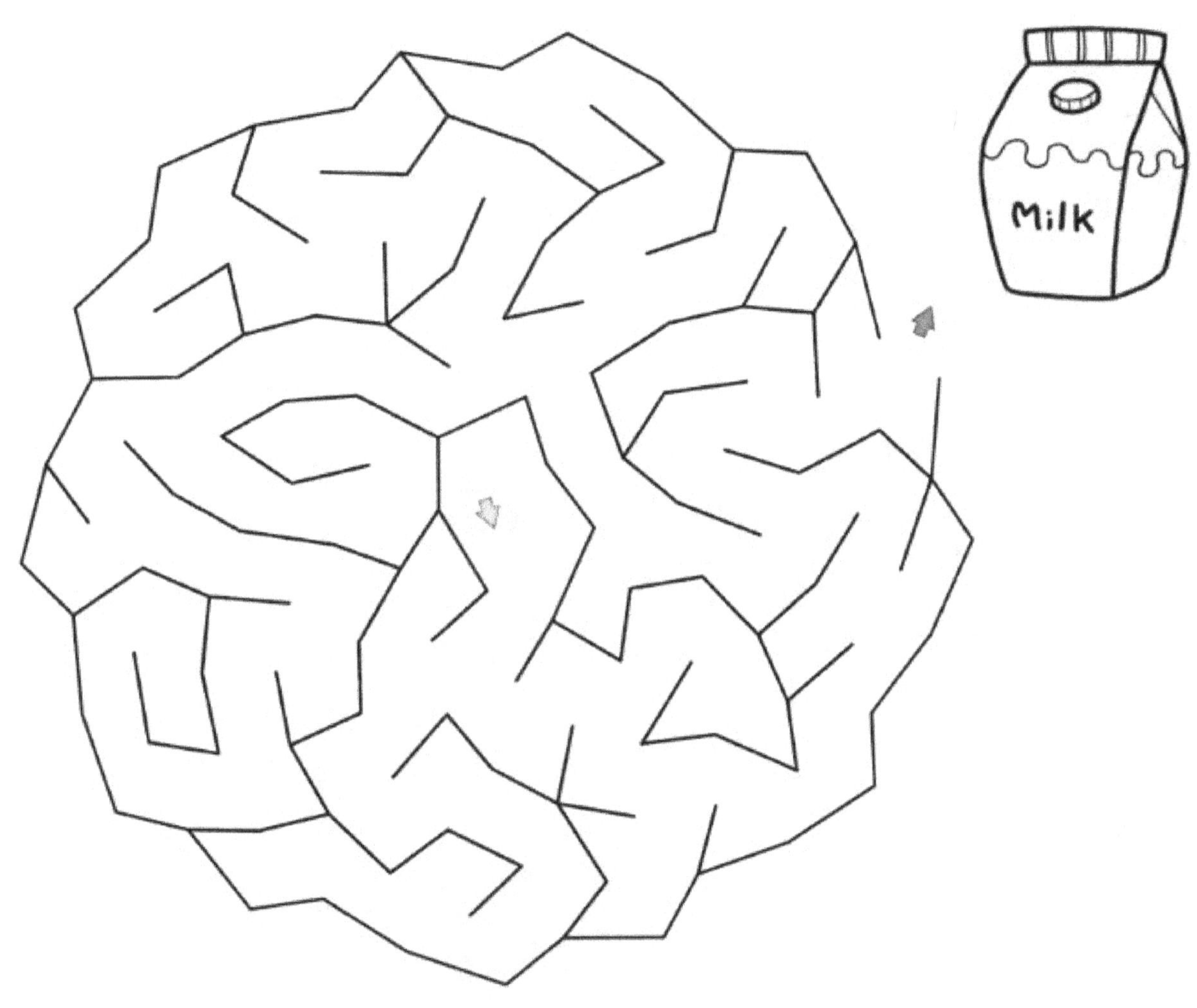
Milk

MILK